I0794721

Outdoor Adventures

Maria Koran

EYEDISCOVER

Go to **www.openlightbox.com** and enter this book's unique code.

BOOK CODE

AVG35349

EYEDISCOVER brings you optic readalongs that support active learning.

Published by Lightbox Learning Inc.
276 5th Avenue, Suite 704 #917
New York, NY 10001
Website: www.openlightbox.com

Copyright ©2023 Lightbox Learning Inc.
All rights reserved. No part of this publication may be reproduced, stored in a retrieval system, or transmitted in any form or by any means, electronic, mechanical, photocopying, recording, or otherwise, without the prior written permission of the publisher.

Library of Congress Control Number: 2022935900

ISBN 978-1-7911-4866-9 (hardcover)
ISBN 978-1-7911-4868-3 (multi-user eBook)

Printed in Guangzhou, China
1 2 3 4 5 6 7 8 9 0 26 25 24 23 22

042022
102121

Project Coordinator: John Willis
Designer: Ana María Vidal

Photo Credits
Every reasonable effort has been made to trace ownership and to obtain permission to reprint copyright material. The publisher would be pleased to have any errors or omissions brought to its attention so that they may be corrected in subsequent printings. The publisher acknowledges Alamy, Getty Images, and Shutterstock as its primary image suppliers for this title.

EYEDISCOVER provides enriched content, optimized for tablet use, that supplements and complements this book. EYEDISCOVER books strive to create inspired learning and engage young minds in a total learning experience.

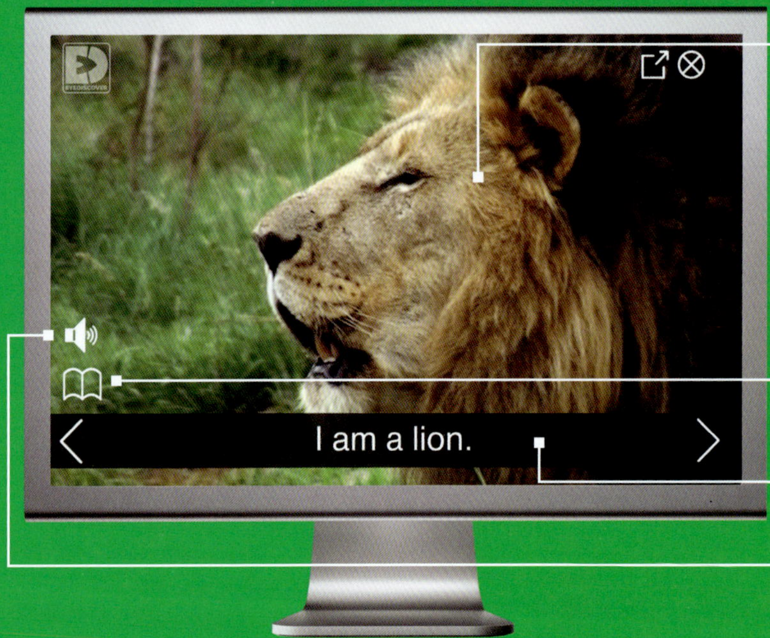

Watch
Video content brings each page to life.

Browse
Thumbnails make navigation simple.

Read
Follow along with text on the screen.

Listen
Hear each page read aloud.

Your EYEDISCOVER Optic Readalongs come alive with...

Audio
Listen to the entire book read aloud.

Video
High resolution videos turn each spread into an optic readalong.

OPTIMIZED FOR
- TABLETS
- WHITEBOARDS
- COMPUTERS
- AND MUCH MORE!

This title is part of our EyeDiscover digital subscription

1-Year EyeDiscover Subscription
ISBN 978-1-4896-8346-5

Access all EyeDiscover titles with our digital subscription.
Sign up for a FREE trial at **www.openlightbox.com/trial**

Outdoor Adventures

In this book, you will learn about

- what they are
- what types there are
- where you have them

and much more!

Many people go on outdoor adventures. They enjoy spending time outside and exercising in nature.

Nature lovers often go camping. They set up a tent or shelter and sleep outdoors.

Hiking is another outdoor activity. Hikers take long walks on paths through nature.

People ride horses on paths, too. Some trips are short. Others can last many days.

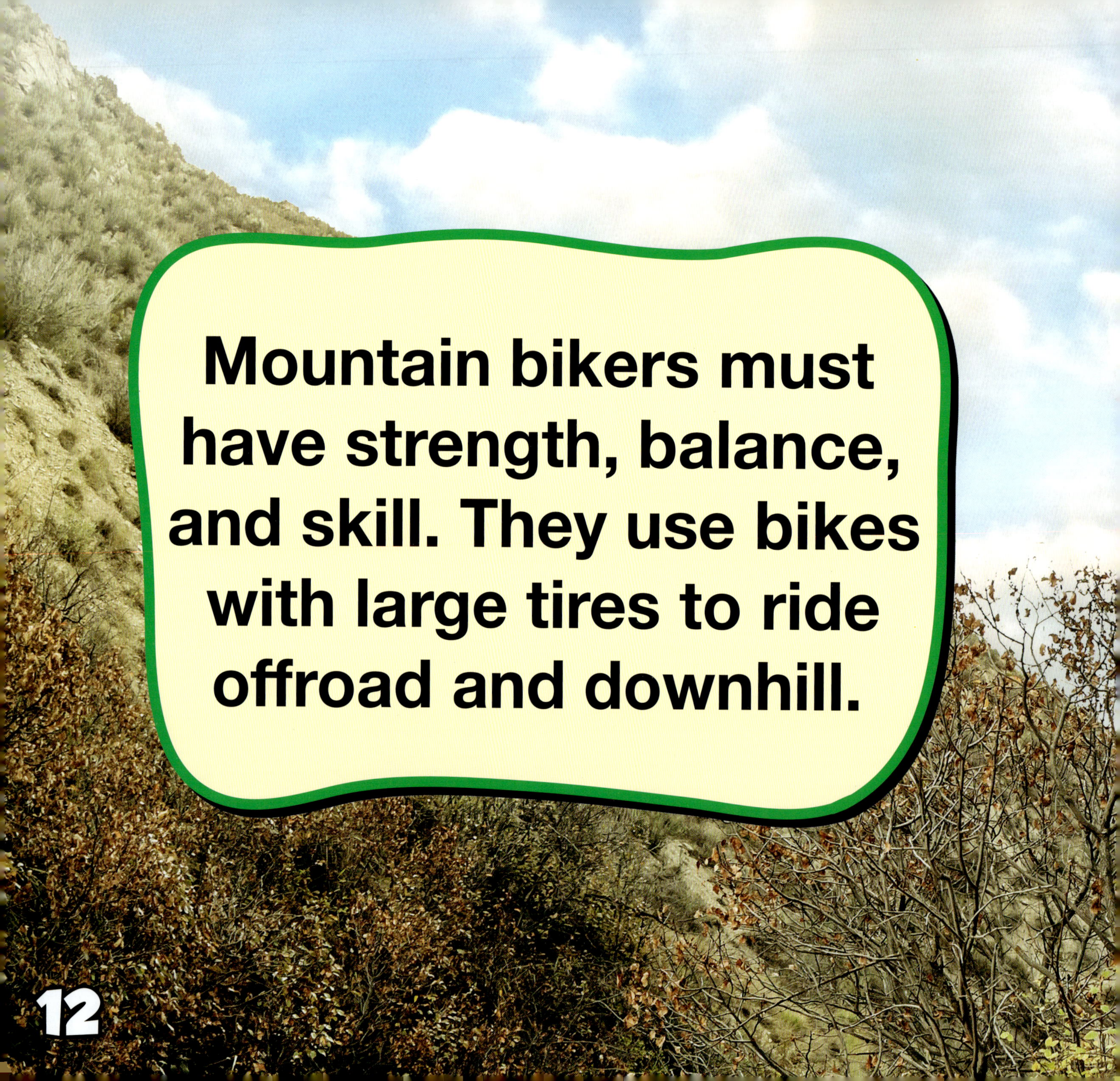

Mountain bikers must have strength, balance, and skill. They use bikes with large tires to ride offroad and downhill.

NRS

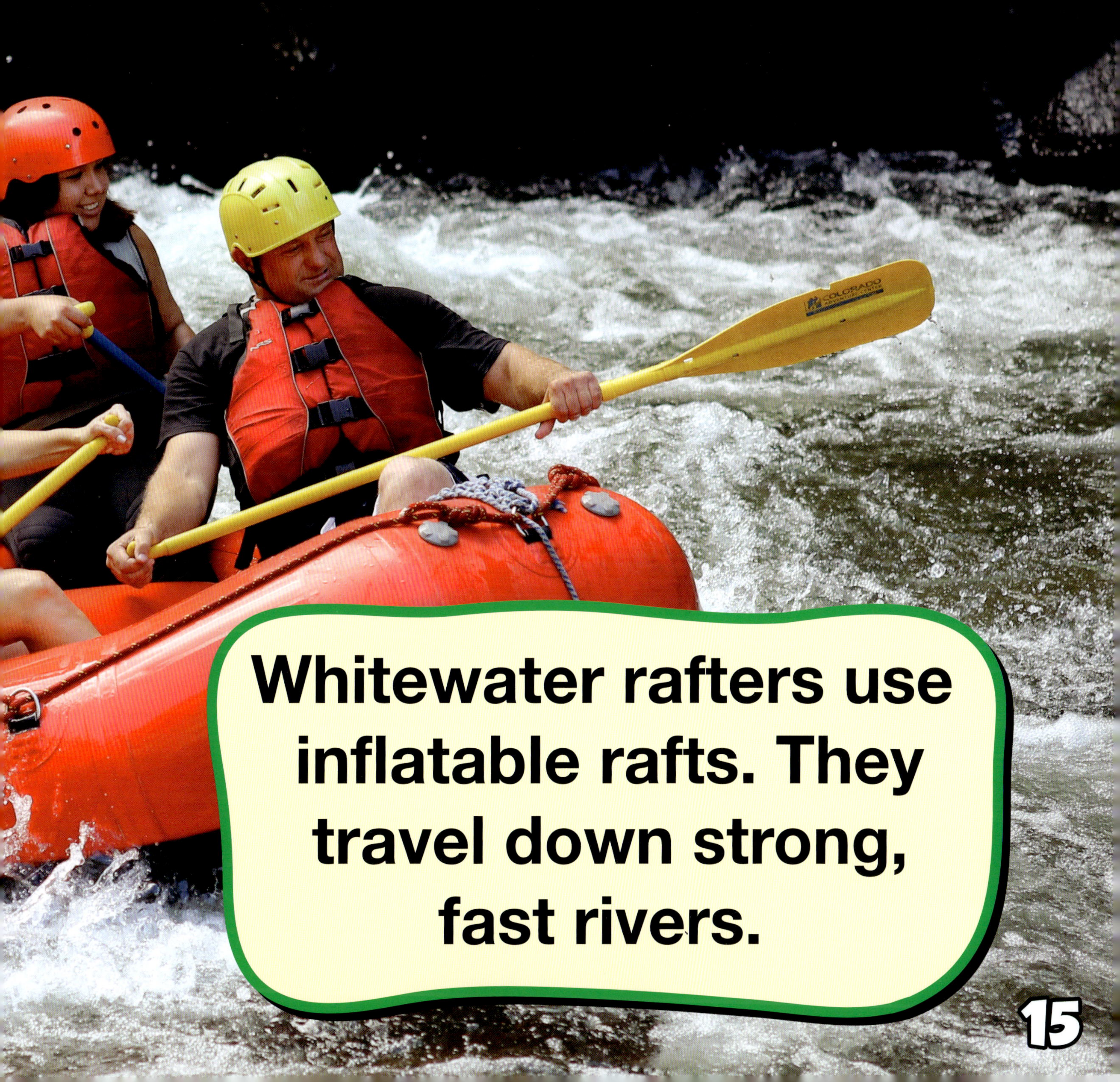

Whitewater rafters use inflatable rafts. They travel down strong, fast rivers.

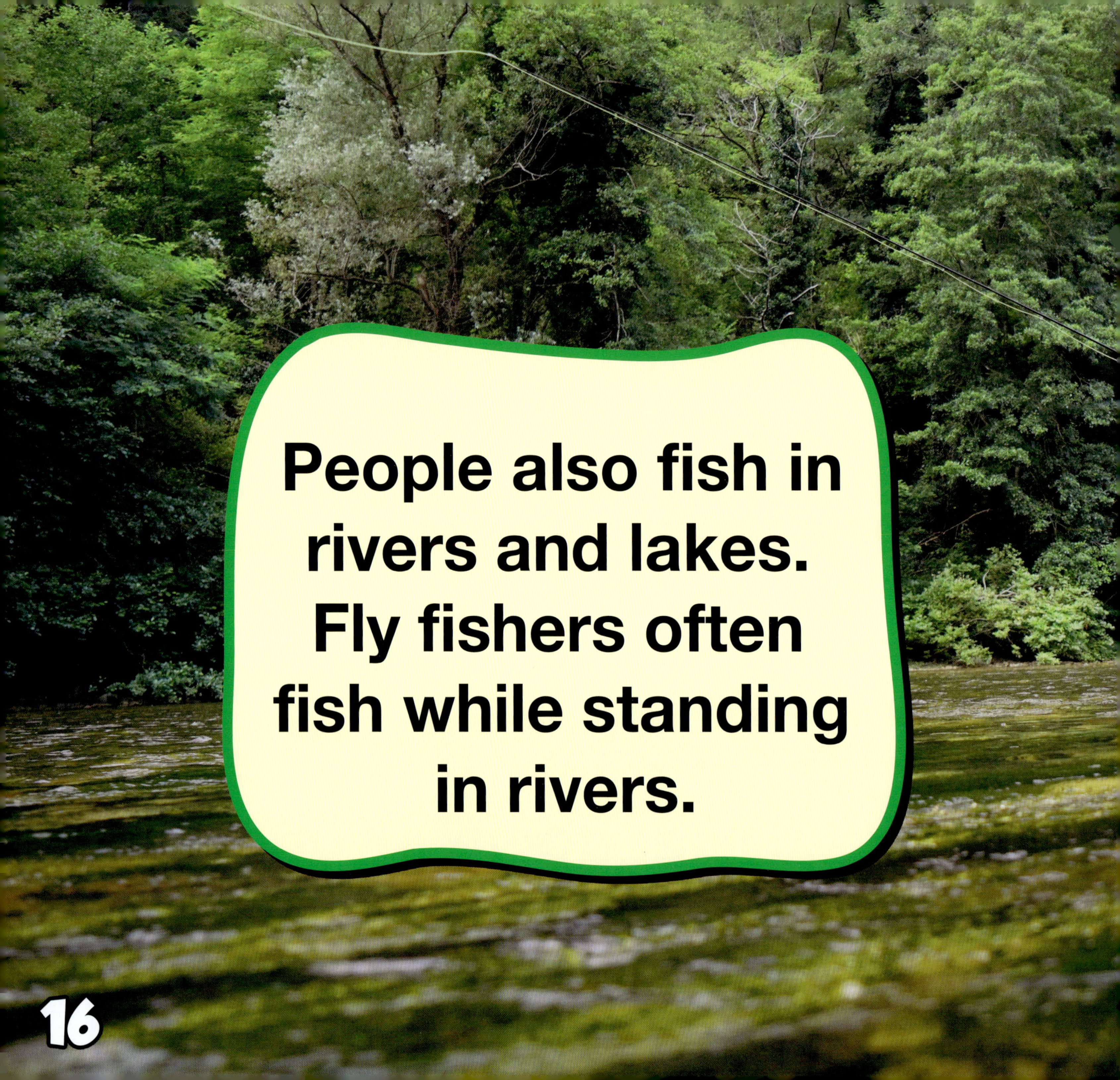

People also fish in rivers and lakes. Fly fishers often fish while standing in rivers.

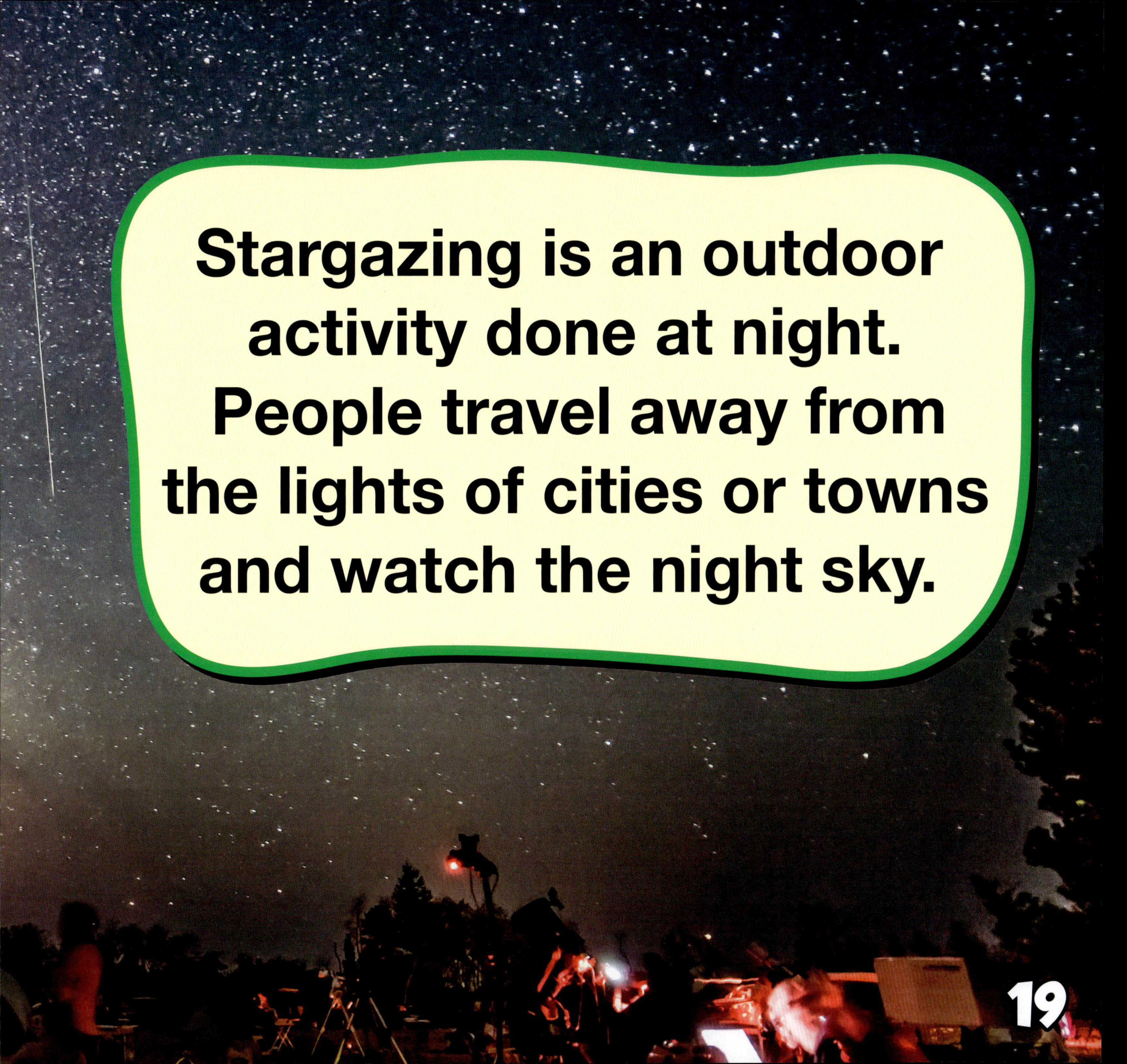

Stargazing is an outdoor activity done at night. People travel away from the lights of cities or towns and watch the night sky.

It is important to clean up any garbage after an outdoor adventure. This helps protect nature for everyone to enjoy.

OUTDOOR ADVENTURES BY THE NUMBERS

About **4 out of 10 campers** in the United States **camp in a state park**.

People have been **riding horses** for more than **5,000 years**.

More than 44 million people go **hiking** in the United States **every year**.

On a **clear night**, away from city lights, a person **can see** more than **2,000 STARS**.

Mountain biking became an **Olympic** event in **1996**.

More than 55 MILLION **Americans fished** in **2020**.

KEY WORDS

Research has shown that as much as 65 percent of all written material published in English is made up of 300 words. These 300 words cannot be taught using pictures or learned by sounding them out. They must be recognized by sight. This book contains 53 common sight words to help young readers improve their reading fluency and comprehension. This book also teaches young readers several important content words, such as proper nouns. These words are paired with pictures to aid in learning and improve understanding.

Page	Sight Words First Appearance
4	and, go, in, many, on, people, they, time
7	a, often, or, set, up
8	another, is, long, take, through, walks
11	are, can, days, last, others, some, too
12	have, large, mountain, must, to, use, with
15	down, rivers
16	also, while
19	an, at, away, from, lights, night, of, the, watch
20	after, any, for, helps, important, it, this

Page	Content Words First Appearance
4	adventures, nature
7	camping, shelter, tent
8	activity, hikers, paths
11	horses, trips
12	balance, bikes, mountain bikers, skill, strength, tires
15	rafts, whitewater rafters
16	fly fishers, lakes
19	sky, stargazing, towns
20	garbage

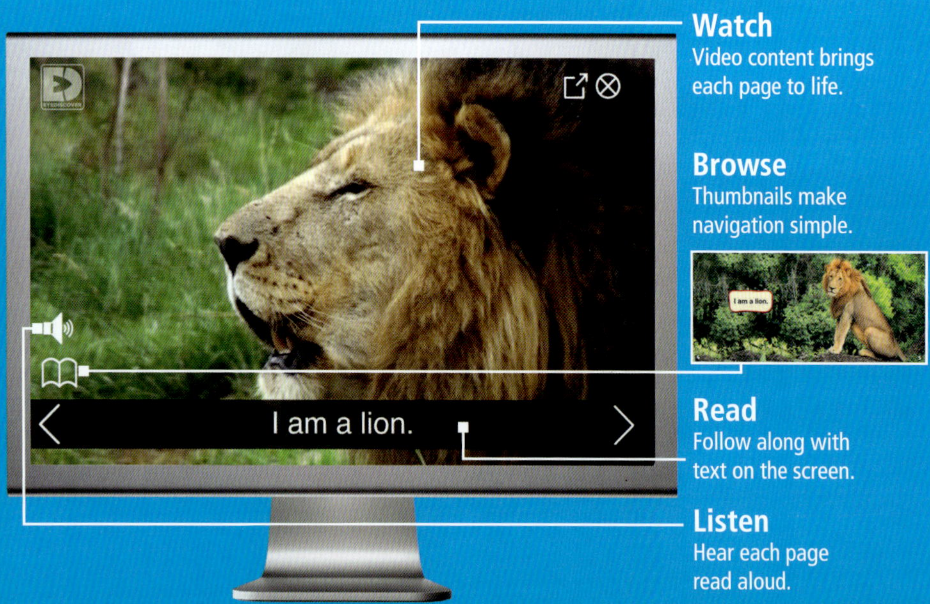

EYEDISCOVER

Go to www.openlightbox.com and enter this book's unique code.

BOOK CODE

AVG35349